Joseph Warren Revere, Library of Congress Pamphlet
Collection

A Statement of the Case of Brigadier-General Joseph W.

Revere

tried by court-marital, and dismissed from the service of the United

States, August 10th, 1863. With a map, a copy of the record of the trial,

and an appendix

Joseph Warren Revere, Library of Congress Pamphlet Collection

A Statement of the Case of Brigadier-General Joseph W. Revere
tried by court-marital, and dismissed from the service of the United States, August 10th, 1863. With a map, a copy of the record of the trial, and an appendix

ISBN/EAN: 9783337733889

Printed in Europe, USA, Canada, Australia, Japan

Cover: Foto ©Suzi / pixelio.de

More available books at **www.hansebooks.com**

A STATEMENT

OF THE CASE OF

BRIGADIER-GENERAL JOSEPH W. REVERE,

UNITED STATES VOLUNTEERS,

TRIED BY COURT-MARTIAL, AND DISMISSED FROM
THE SERVICE OF THE UNITED STATES,
AUGUST 10TH, 1863.

WITH

A MAP, A COPY OF THE RECORD OF THE TRIAL, AND AN APPENDIX.

NEW YORK:
PRINTED BY C. A. ALVORD.
1863.

PREFACE.

JUSTICE to those friends and fellow-citizens of mine, at whose instance I took up arms in this war, and also to a military reputation founded upon twenty-five years spent in the service of the United States, in her armies and in the Navy, in every part of the world, compels me to lay before those friends and the public, the following statement of facts and accompanying documents.

I have endeavored to confine myself strictly to the official action of the Court-Martial which sentenced me to dismissal from the Army, and to matters respecting that action; for, in my quality of a soldier, I have always judged men by their acts, and not by what they say of themselves, or by what their friends or others say of them.

I submit this statement in the belief that the public, more fully informed than the Court, will exonerate me from the censure cast upon me by its sentence.

J. W. REVERE.

THE WILLOWS, NEAR MORRISTOWN, N. J.
September, 1863.

STATEMENT.

At a General Court-Martial, ordered by General HOOKER, commanding the Army of the Potomac, held near Falmouth, Virginia, on the 12th day of May, 1863, for the trial of Brigadier-General JOSEPH W. REVERE, United States Volunteers, the following charges were preferred by General SICKLES, commanding the Third Corps:

FIRST CHARGE.—Misbehavior before the enemy.

Specification.—In this, that Brigadier-General J. W. Revere, United States Volunteers, commanding Third Excelsior (Second) Brigade, Second Division, Third Corps, while the said division was engaged with the enemy at Chancellorsville, Virginia, did march his command an unnecessary distance to the rear to re-form it, and did then march with his brigade, and such fragments of other regiments of the said division as he could assemble, to United States Ford, about five miles from the scene of action. All this without orders from his superior officers, about eight o'clock on the morning of May 3d, 1863.

CHARGE SECOND.—Neglect of duty, to the prejudice of good order and military discipline.

Specification.—In this, that Brigadier-General J. W. Revere, United States Volunteers, commanding Excelsior (Second) Brigade, Second Division, Third Corps, did allow public property to the amount of 189 muskets, 178 sets of accoutrements, 259 bayonets, 28,440 rounds of small-arm ammunition, 1,779 knapsacks, 836 haversacks, 494 canteens, 2,000 shelter tents, and fifty-five pioneer tools, in the service of his command, to be abandoned, and to fall into the hands of the enemy. All this without orders from his superior officers at Chancellorsville, Virginia, on or about May 3d, 1863.

And the finding of the Court was in these terms:

Of the Specification to First Charge, guilty, except the words, "while said division was engaged with the enemy at Chancellorsville, Virginia, did march his command an unnecessary distance to the rear to re-form it, "and" "then" and "to United States Ford, about five miles from the scene.of action," substituting for the latter clause, "to about three miles from the scene of action, towards United States Ford."

Of the First Charge, not guilty, but guilty of conduct to the prejudice of good order and military discipline.

Of the Specification to Second Charge, not guilty.

Of Second Charge, not guilty.

The finding on the First Specification, then, is as follows:

Guilty, in this, "that Brigadier-General J. W. REVERE, United States Volunteers, commanding Excelsior (Second) Brigade, Second Division, Third Corps, did march with his brigade, and such fragments of other regiments of the said division as he could assemble, to about three miles from the scene of action, towards United States Ford."

The sentence of the Court was, that General Revere be dismissed from the military service of the United States.

This sentence was approved by the President on the 10th day of August, 1863, and made known to the accused on the 15th day of August, 1863.

I.

The Court-Martial held the grave charges of neglect of duty and misbehavior before the enemy to be unfounded, and rested its sentence upon the far less disgraceful charge of "conduct to the prejudice of good order and military discipline." I make no comment upon the spirit which dictated an accusation fatal, if proved, to the honor of a brother soldier, yet unsustained by the facts: nor is it necessary to dwell on that large portion of the evidence in the case which relates to the second charge. The reader is capable of deciding for himself in what degree the facts warrant the finding, and to what extent the finding justifies the severity of the sentence.

No defence was offered by the accused on the trial. At the close of the case for the prosecution, my counsel, General D. B. Birney, was so entirely satisfied with the evidence, as exonerating me from all censure, that, after offering the testimony of two officers for the defence, in explanation of some details, he advised the course of submitting the case to the Court, without making any argument, or any fuller explanation of the circumstances and motives governing my action. It was his opinion, as well as that of my friends present at the trial, that the case for the prosecution had completely broken down; and I received their congratulations upon the result, without a doubt of my acquittal. Nor were any of us prepared for the extraordinary course which the Court adopted, in pronouncing me not guilty upon both the charges, yet framing another charge, fitting a part of one of the original specifications to it, and condemning me thus, in fact, unheard upon that particular accusation. "Neglect of duty," under the second charge, we were prepared to disprove, and did in fact disprove, by the very evidence for the prosecution. The more general charge of " conduct prejudicial to good order and military discipline" required a different defence, resting upon motives, upon special information, and reasons for action, known only to the accused; and, if it had been fairly presented, it would have been met by such a defence. How far the Court was justified by military law in this peculiar finding, will be inquired in another part of this paper.

Some confusion may have been produced in the minds of the members of the Court, by the ingenuity with which the chief witnesses for the prosecution insinuated the proof of an offence not really charged. Their testimony labors to establish two facts; one supporting the charges, and the other wholly irrelevant to them. The first is the offence of misconduct while commanding the division ; the other, that of misconduct in unwarrantably assuming command of it. Now, while the latter, if proved, could have had no effect upon the case as charged, it might very easily have fixed upon the minds of the Court an impression of insubordination, which must have affected their finding. No evidence was offered by me to disturb this erroneous impression. An attentive reader of the testimony can hardly escape the conclusion, that the false issue thus craftily presented may have had this effect.

II.

Some explanation of earlier events and circumstances is necessary for a clear understanding of the questions with which the Court had to deal.

First, as to the command of my division.

The three brigades composing the Second Division of the Third Corps, were commanded respectively by Brigadier-General Mott, in command of the Third Brigade ; Brigadier-General Revere, in command of the Second ; and Acting Brigadier-General Carr, in command of the First. The numbering of these brigades has no reference to the relative rank of their respective commanders. General Mott and myself were commissioned Brigadier-Generals, his commission bearing date in September, 1862, and mine in October, 1862. Brigadier-General Carr had been appointed to that rank by the President in September, 1862, but the Senate had not confirmed his appointment. After the adjournment of Congress, and in March, 1863, he was reappointed by the President, and it was under that appointment only, dated in March, 1863, and giving him rank from that time, that he was an acting Brigadier-General at the battle of Chancellorsville. His original date had not then been given him. This appointment was afterwards cancelled, and a new one, antedated, given him. (See testimony of Sickles.) Some time after the return of the army, from the campaign of the early days of May, to the camp near Falmouth, he did there receive from the President an appointment, dated back to the original one of September, 1862; but he had not in May, nor has he now, a commission confirmed by the Senate. Thus neither by date of commission, nor by that of appointment, could he have ranked me. That he acquiesced, with others, in this view of his position, is clear from the fact that at all reviews, marches, &c., of the Second Division, Third Corps, he was placed junior to both myself and General Mott; nor was either of us ever informed, by General Sickles or General Hooker, that any other claim as to rank for General Carr was made, either by him or them, until it was announced, just after the battle of Chancellorsville, that General Carr was in command of our division.

Next, as to the occurrences which led to the situation at the time referred to in the charges.

The operations in which my brigade took part, during the few days preceding the battle of May 3d, at Chancellorsville, were peculiarly harassing and fatiguing. (See Appendix II.) After several days continuous marching and countermarching, near Falmouth, on the north bank of the Rappahannock, the brigade crossed that river on Friday, the 1st day of May, and moved to the front at Chancellorsville, where they were stationed as a reserve, to support the troops then hotly engaged, and where, that night, they bivouacked under arms. It will be recollected, that during that night and the following day the enemy were busy in cutting a road through the forest, around our left flank and along our front, and in marching by it immense masses from our left to our right, in preparation for the furious attack made from the westward towards Saturday evening, the 2d of May. The Second Division, after being under arms the whole of Saturday, were hurried forward about 5 P. M.

to check this assault, and to restore the battle, which was fast turning into a rout, from the repulse of the Eleventh Corps, which had given way on the extreme right. During the night between Saturday and Sunday, the brigade, while kept constantly on the alert from frequent alarms and the driving in of pickets, managed to throw up a line of log breastworks, expecting a renewal of the attack, for which we knew the enemy were massing their forces. The last communication I had with General Sickles was through General Berry, about two o'clock on Saturday afternoon, and the only food my men received was at noon of that day—rest they had none. Going towards the rear during the night, I discovered that we had no second line there, and that our right was uncovered—a distance of half a mile, unoccupied by troops, intervening between it and the next force, at White House.

That night we took prisoners a captain and some twenty privates of the enemy, from whom we learned that General A. P. Hill commanded a large force directly in our front, intending to attack and gain possession of the cross-roads at Chancellorsville; and that Stonewall Jackson had already thrown heavy masses of infantry and artillery towards our extreme right, and intended to force his way at early morning between our army and the river. This most important information was at once sent to General Berry, my immediate chief; but whether it was forwarded by him to the generals of corps, or the general-in-chief, I do not know. (See Appendix III.)

At daylight on Sunday, May 3d, the enemy drove in our pickets, and opened the battle with a heavy fire of artillery and musketry. The brigade fought steadily for several hours, until the enemy turned our left flank, and enfiladed the breastwork, when they were forced by numbers to retire.

A few words explanatory of the map prefixed will complete this sketch of the position and the circumstances in which, at eight o'clock on the morning of Sunday, May 3d, I adopted, with deliberate judgment, and from a conviction of duty, the course which is condemned by this sentence as a military crime.

The country in which the battle of Chancellorsville was fought is a plain, overgrown with dense woods, through which a road runs southwardly from the United States Ford of the Rappahannock, intersected, at the hamlet of Chancellorsville, by a plank-road running westwardly from Fredericksburg to Orange Court-House. This crossing-place it was essential to the safety of Lee's army to hold, and accordingly they had, as stated, during Friday and Saturday, cut a road through the woods completely around our left flank and along our front, and had attacked us from the west with an immense force under their best leaders. Pushing this bold movement still further north towards the river, they confronted our army with a powerful line which stretched in a general direction parallel to its front, and to the road leading to United States Ford, threatening that vital point in our communications. It is clear then that, in a general sense, the " scene of action" became the whole extent of this road, from Chancellorsville to the river, and that the peril and the chance of conflict was no greater on our left than on our right, where the onset of Jackson might at any moment be expected. The distance from Chancellorsville to the White House is about three-quarters of a mile ; from Chancellorsville to the ford is not less than four miles ; and from the point to which my shattered brigade withdrew on Sunday morning, to the ford, is about three miles and a half. In the neighborhood of the White House the forest thins out to a small clearing of about ten acres ; and around the brick house near the ford is a much larger open space, while between these two points the woods are dense. The open space around the White House was crowded on the morning of Sunday, after the action, with troops moving in both directions, stragglers going to the rear, and artillery and infantry arriving constantly and debouching into it. It was also occupied by the fresh troops of (I think) the Second Corps. Such was the crowd and want of space, that I was requested by several staff officers, one

an A. D. C. of the general staff, to remove my troops in order
to make room.

III,

Into this crowded spot, then, the only open one within some
miles, we had been driven in disorder and complete disorgani-
zation after the engagement of Sunday morning, there being
no second line of battle in our immediate rear, behind which
we might rally. I collected here five or six hundred men of
the different regiments of the division, who had straggled in
after the action. The senior officer in command at that point
being General French, I reported myself to him, and received
from him the advice to occupy with my men a line of abatis
(designated on the map as Fig. 1). These, however, I found
filled with troops, leaving no room for the addition of mine.
Here, at this time, I heard from his A. D. C. of the death of
General Berry, my division commander, who was killed at
about half-past seven o'clock ; and immediately afterwards I
met Brigadier-General Mott, the next in seniority in the division, going to the rear, severely wounded. I at once conclud-
ed that I was the commanding officer of the Second Division,
Third Corps ; and in that capacity I directed all the officers of
my division who could be found, personally and through my
staff, to rally and report to me. And as this new position
devolved upon me both the responsibility of directing the division, and the enlarged discretion which every general officer in
such circumstances is supposed to possess, I determined upon
my course of action, in view of all the facts which have been
stated.

The need of some action was urgent. I believed myself to
be the division commander. I had had no communication
with my corps commander since noon of the preceding day,
nor was any now possible. Nothing could be heard of him or

of his staff from the numerous stragglers of the Third Corps, who were constantly passing us to the rear, through the woods flanking the road. I knew only that he had been engaged in the same action with ourselves, and supposed that he had shared the same disorganizing repulse. To reunite my small force to him, through the inextricable crowds passing confusedly in both directions between us and the front, would have been impossible, even had his head-quarters been fixed or known. My men were worn with the marches and battles of four days, with want of rest and food for the last twenty-four hours, and with sharp fighting for the last four, and were nearly out of ammunition. Stragglers from all the regiments of the corps were passing in increasing numbers, adding constantly to the force which could only be collected by retiring, and could not have been re-formed, if present, where we were. Add to this, that with my mind full of the intelligence received from the prisoners of the last night, I was convinced that there might be use for troops anywhere along the road to the ford; that the front of the battle had indeed been shifted far to the right; and that a large portion of the division, reorganized, refreshed, and resupplied, would be of more service there than a few hundred men could be, standing faint and idle where we were, or vainly striving to cross the torrent flowing past them. Or, if not needed at the right, surely the time would not be wasted which should be devoted to placing them in such force and condition that they could be marched back again to join in the battle which had ceased in our front, and which would meantime be sustained by fresh troops, if renewed during our absence. It was not so renewed, nor were we ever so far from the point we had left that it could not have been reached in a reasonable time.

My duty was to collect my division and bring it, ready for action, into union with its corps. Had I at that moment received any orders, they would have been the same which the corps commander states in his evidence that he gave to other general officers—to report with my command. This could only be done by overtaking and rallying its débris, as they streamed towards the point where alone rest, and food, and ammunition, and space to form could be gained, and where, as I at least knew, a chance of early action was to be looked for also; and then returning with it towards head-quarters, which would by that time be established and accessible. At this moment they were not fixed, for Sickles states that only after Berry's death was the movement made for this purpose. I therefore, in the absence of orders, after reflection, sensible of the responsibility involved, but confident that it was the only course for bringing my troops speedily into efficient service, determined upon the movement for which I am censured by the Court.

Striking a direct course by compass through the woods, I moved a mile and a quarter towards a point on the main road about midway to the United States Ford, and then marched a short distance down the main road, to a position where the stragglers on both sides of it might be intercepted and rallied, and where orders from either flank might reach us with equal ease. Arrived at this point, I halted the column, sent out patrols in all directions, to collect stragglers, and obtained from the river, and distributed, food and ammunition. During this time I saw several general officers, and at least one major-general, engaged in the same duty of rallying troops, who filled the whole space between my position and the river, in a vast and confused throng. At this time and place too I saw and spoke with Lieutenant-Colonel O. H. Hart, Adjutant-General to General Sickles, who with two aides was busy in the same work. At noon reports were called for from the different regiments, and 1,715 officers and men, in the aggregate, were reported present for duty. Anxious to avoid delay, I gave the men but little time to prepare their food, and then led the division towards the front again, increasing our force at every rod. Hearing while on the march that the Third Brigade was collected close to the ford, I sent one of my aides, Lieutenant Belger, to bring them up. Being thus joined by over three hundred men more, gathered from the different divisions of the Third Corps, I continued the movement to the front. When within half a mile of General Sickles's bivouac, on this return march, I received orders (the first that were received by me from any one whatever during that day) by an aide from him, directing me to return, and shortly after an order to the same effect from General Carr was handed to me. Major Burns testifies that he also met on this march an aide from General Sickles, with orders to do exactly what we were doing—bring the stragglers to the front.

I reached the front at the head of about 2,000 men of the division, at half-past two in the afternoon, by my watch. I reported here to General Sickles, who relieved me of my command. I at once offered to serve as a volunteer in any capacity, in the battle that seemed impending. My request was refused, and General Sickles demanded an explanation, which I gave in writing. (Appendix IV.)

It is here that I positively deny having ever sent an aide, or orderly, or any other messenger to General Carr, with orders to him to report to me at or near the United States Ford, as that officer has stated in his testimony on the trial.

To sum up all in a few words,—after the fight was ended, left without orders, and crowded off the field, I led away a handful of worn and disorganized men towards a point where, in my belief, an action might even then be going on, and brought them back within six hours, after retiring less than three miles, two thousand strong, refreshed and resupplied. Was this a breach of duty?

IV.

If the reader will now compare the original charges with the evidence on the record, and will also compare the finding of the Court with the facts as above stated, he may see reason to conclude that as the charges were not supported by the case made for the prosecution, so the finding would not have been justified if the matters just narrated had been offered by way of defence, fortified, as they could have been, by ample proof. For what is the substance of the finding? Let it be borne in mind that, by the law of courts-martial, "a prisoner must be acquitted or convicted of every part of each of the several specifications and charges of which he stands accused."* The Court then acquits me of those parts of the original specification to the first charge which in the finding are "excepted" from the conclusion of "guilty"—acquits me of "marching my command while engaged with the enemy"—acquits me of "marching an unnecessary distance to the rear." What is left in the finding thus emasculated? The simple fact that I "marched with the Second Brigade, and such fragments of other regiments of the division as could be assembled, to about three miles from the scene of action, towards the United States Ford"—a fact in itself indifferent, implying no criminality nor neglect, and deriving its character only from the attendant circumstances and motives. I have shown from these circumstances and motives that the intention was right, and the act advisable. Something was required, beyond the facts so found, to give my conduct the character of a military offence. I believe that incriminating element is to be found in the false impression on the minds of the Court, not derived from the charges, but artfully suggested by the principal witnesses, uncontradicted by me, and leaving its traces in the finding—the impression that I wrongfully assumed the command of the division. That would indeed warrant the finding of "conduct to the prejudice of discipline and good order." The reader can decide what the Court had no opportunity of doing, how innocent I am of this offence.

But the peculiar finding of the Court suggests a far graver question, as to the regularity and lawfulness of their mode of proceeding. The objection I here make is not one of techni-

---

* Benét on Courts-Martial, pp. 126, 129. De Hart, p. 172.

cality, but one which, if well founded, vitiates and renders illegal the whole finding and sentence. It rests upon principles of military law, arising in former cases, and settled by decisions recorded in the War Department.

By the rules and practice of courts-martial, military charges must be brought under some one or other of the Articles of War. When the specified facts and circumstances clearly point to a particular Article, the prosecution must be had under that Article, and the charge expressed in the terms used therein.* Besides the various particular Articles of War, which assign a penalty for definite and specified offences, there is an Article known as the General Article (No. 99), which provides for the trial of all crimes not capital, and all disorders and neglects to the prejudice of good order and military discipline ; and any offence not specifically provided for must be charged under this General Article. Accordingly, in my case, the first charge, that of misbehavior before the enemy was specifically brought under Article 52, which provides for that offence ; and the second charge, that of neglect of duty, an offence not provided for in any specific article, was brought under the General Article (99). The Court acquitted me on both charges ; but then proceeded to frame a new charge, to connect with it a part of the specification to the first charge, under Article 52, and to pronounce a finding of "guilty," under Article 99. This it was beyond their lawful power to do. A court-martial, after the prisoner is arraigned, cannot alter or amend the original charges, nor entertain additional ones.† It must be remembered that charge and specification number two were both dismissed ; they were disposed of, and were no longer in the case, and the only question was as to what the finding should be on the first specification. The law, as settled by the highest authority, the War Department, in the cases to which I have referred, holds that where a charge is laid under a specific Article, the accused must be found guilty of a violation of

* Benét, p. 53. De Hart, p. 298.   † Benét, p. 91. De Hart, 102.

2

that article, or be acquitted. The court cannot find him guilty
of the specification as an offence under the 99th Article.* "It
is necessary that the offence against the 99th Article should be
duly and regularly charged, in order that the accused may
have notice of that which he is to answer. A charge of one of
the specific offences defined in other articles is not notice of a
general charge of some disorder or neglect within the 99th
Article."† In another case, where the charge was made under
Article 83, the decision says: "The court have acquitted the
accused of the legal charge against him. At the same time
they give judgment against him under the 99th Article of War.
He was not charged with any offence under that Article. If
charges are so drawn as to bring them expressly and exclusively
under particular Articles of War, a court-martial cannot con-
vict under other Articles. The sentence of the court-martial in
this case is therefore void."‡

Again, in a case still nearer to the present, it is said : "The
court find the prisoner guilty of the specification to the first
charge, and not guilty of the first charge, and not guilty of the
second charge and its specification, and do sentence him, &c.
The proceedings of the court in this case are disapproved; the
court, although finding a part of the facts alleged against the
prisoner, having acquitted him of both the charges preferred,
proceeded irregularly in passing sentence upon him."§

Nor can it be said that the Court here proceeded, in the exer-
cise of that discretion which military law allows it, to substitute
in the finding 'a less degree of the offence charged. That
discretion is limited to the choice between offences of a kindred
nature. But cowardice, which is the essence of the charge of
misbehavior before the enemy, is a crime that stands single,
and admits no shades of shame. There is no other offence of
which it is an aggravated form. Between' it and conduct to
the prejudice of good order and discipline the difference is one

---

* Benét, 130.

† General Orders, War Department, No. 7, June 18, 1856.

‡ General Orders, War Department, No. 8, July 23, 1856.

§ General Orders, Head-Quarters of the Army, No. 69, Dec. 30, 1843.

of kind, and not of degree ; and it is not lawful for a court to adopt a difference of that nature as a basis on which to construct its finding.*

On this high authority I impeach the finding, and protest against the sentence of the Court-Martial in my case, as illegal, and exceeding the power of the tribunal.

V,

I have turned with reluctance from the merits of the case to a discussion of its form, and now proceed, with still greater unwillingness, to speak of some personal considerations. It is a painful necessity which compels an officer, thus dragged into public view for branding, to risk the blame of egotism by doing violence to his natural feelings of reserve. But the justice to myself and others, which prompts this statement, demands that it should be complete.

Having received, from my own and other countries, testimonials, to me priceless, of my behavior as a soldier, I can smile at the flagrant vindictiveness of a charge which imputes to me cowardice on the field. But to the public, usually only half informed through the newspapers, the opinion of those lately my companions in arms may be of value. (Appendix V.) The Court threw this charge aside, as it deserved, adopting, instead, the different and milder one of breach of discipline.

If it is difficult to make the finding of the Court consistent with law and evidence, it is still more difficult to reconcile either with the extreme harshness of the sentence. I am too old a soldier not to be aware that stern examples are needed in all armies, and that a general officer must sometimes suffer for errors of judgment in discharging the responsibilities which duty casts upon him. But some proportion should be observed between the offence and the penalty ; and, in all armies, length

* Benét, p. 132.

of service, wounds, and imprisonment, may be pleaded in
mitigation of punishment; and personal character may be
made the ground of an appeal to the lenity of a court.

· The greater part of my life has been devoted, in the profession
of arms, to the service of my country, following naturally the
traditions of a family which gave one not undistinguished
name to the Revolutionary War, and which has offered two
other of its members to death for the State, in this one. I
have been for thirty years a sailor and a soldier. Had I been
a politician in epaulettes, plying in the camp the arts of the
caucus, and cking out by chicane defects in soldiership; or had
I been lifted from some low employment to a rank won only
by servility, and held only by pliancy, there might be retribu-
tive, though indirect, justice in this sentence. But I have
been more versed in war than in intrigue. On all that Court,
eminent as most of its members were, there was not one who
was not my junior in length of employment in the United
States service. I am censured for conduct to the prejudice of
discipline, after having served for twenty years, under the iron
discipline of the old navy, without a reproach on that score—
after having held in Mexico, in 1851, the rank of lieutenant-
colonel, and instructor of artillery, conferred in view of my
fitness as a disciplinarian—after being appointed a brigadier-
general of volunteers, on the recommendation of General
Hooker himself, founded expressly on my known experience
in discipline, and justified, before and since, by the severe and
exact enforcement of that military virtue, for which I am well
known in our present army, and which has borne its fruits in
the brilliant reputation of the 7th New Jersey Volunteers, trained
and originally commanded by me*—after having served in
the battles of the Peninsula, during the campaign of Pope, and
at Fredericksburg, with wounds, but without a blemish upon
my military character, in that or any other respect. Surely,
the testimony of such a record to the improbability of the

---

* This regiment, at the battle of Chancellorsville, captured five regimental colors
and 360 prisoners, a larger number than the force they took into the action.

offence, should have outweighed all but the most direct and absolute proof that it was committed. At least, with such a record, I had a right to expect from the Court, even with my defence unheard, greater lenity than is shown in this cruel sentence—and from the President, even though his attention scarcely rested upon my case, some indulgence for one who has given the prime of his life, without military reproach hitherto, to the service of the State. Upon that record, and this Statement, asking only an impartial hearing, I invoke the judgment of that public opinion to which all are amenable, and which seldom fails, in the end, to do justice.

APPENDIX I.

Proceedings of a General Court-Martial.

Major-General W. S. HANCOCK, U. S. V., *President.*
Lieutenant-Colonel E. R. PLATT, *Judge Advocate.*
Brigadier-General Jos. W. REVERE, U. S. V., *Prisoner tried.*
Official copy for Brigadier-General JOSEPH W. REVERE, U. S. Vols.

A. A. HOSMER, Captain 14th Mass. Vols.,
Assistant to Judge Advocate General.

Proceedings of a General Court-Martial which convened at Head-Quarters Third Corps, by virtue of the following orders, viz :

HEAD-QUARTERS ARMY OF THE POTOMAC,
CAMP NEAR FALMOUTH, VA., *May 12th*, 1863.

SPECIAL ORDERS, No. 128.

5. A General Court-Martial is hereby appointed to meet at the Head-Quarters Second Brigade, Second Division, Third Corps, at 10 o'clock A. M. on Wednesday, the 13th day of May, 1863, or as soon thereafter as practicable, for the trial of Brigadier-General Jos. W. REVERE, Volunteer service ; and such other prisoners as may be brought before it.

Detail for the Court.

1. Major-General W. S. HANCOCK, Volunteer Service.
2.   "   "   JOHN NEWTON,   "   "
3. Brig'r.-General JAS. S. WADSWORTH, "   "
4.   "   "   W. T. H. BROOKS,   "   "
5.   "   "   A. A. HUMPHREYS,   "   "
6.   "   "   JOHN GIBBON,   "   "
7.   "   "   FRAS. C. BARLOW,   "   "
8.   "   "   R. B. AYRES,   "   "
9.   "   "   S. K. ZOOK,   "   "

Lieutenant-Colonel E. R. PLATT, Capt. 2d Artillery,
Judge Advocate.

No other officers than those named can be assembled without manifest injury to the service. The Court will sit without regard to hours.

The Chief Quartermaster of the Third Corps will provide necessary accommodations for the assembling of the Court.

By command of Major-General HOOKER.

(Signed) S. WILLIAMS, *Asst. Adjutant-General.*

HEAD-QUARTERS ARMY OF THE POTOMAC,
CAMP NEAR FALMOUTH, VA., *May* 12*th*, 1863.

SPECIAL ORDERS, No. 128.

EXTRACT.

8. The General Court-Martial appointed by paragraph 5, Special Orders of this date, will meet at the Head-Quarters of the Third Corps, instead of at the Head-Quarters Second Brigade, Second Division, as therein directed.

*　　　*　　　*　　　*　　　*　　　*

•　　　　　　By command of Major-General HOOKER.

(Signed) S. WILLIAMS, *Asst. Adjutant-General.*

HEAD-QUARTERS THIRD CORPS,
10.30 A. M., *May* 13*th*, 1863.

Court met pursuant to the foregoing orders.

Present.

1.	Major-General	W. S. HANCOCK,	Volunteer Service.
2.	" "	JOHN NEWTON,	" "
3.	Brig'r.-General	JAS. S. WADSWORTH,	" "
4.	" "	W. T. H. BROOKS,	" "
5.	" "	A. A. HUMPHREYS,	" "
6.	" "	JOHN GIBBON,	" "
7.	" "	FRAS. C. BARLOW,	" "
8.	" "	R. B. AYRES,	" "
9.	" "	S. K. ZOOK,	" "

Lieutenant-Colonel E. R. PLATT, *Judge Advocate*, also present.

Brigadier-General Jos. W. REVERE, U. S. Volunteers, the accused, was called into Court, and having heard the order assembling the Court read, was asked if he objected to any member mentioned therein—to which he replied in the negative. The Court was then duly sworn, in the presence of the accused, by the Judge Advocate, and the Judge Advocate was duly sworn, in the presence of the accused, by the presiding officer.

Brigadier-General Jos. W. REVERE, U. S. Volunteers, was then arraigned on the following Charges and *Specifications:*

CHARGE 1st.—Misbehavior before the enemy.

Specification.—In this, that Brigadier-General J. W. REVERE, U. S. Volunteers, commanding Excelsior (Second) Brigade, Second Division, Third Corps, while said division was engaged with the enemy at Chancellorsville, Virginia, did march his command an unnecessary distance to the rear to reform it, and did then march with his brigade, and such fragments of other regiments of the said division as he could assemble, to United States Ford, about five miles from the scene of action.

All this without orders from his superior officers, about 8 o'clock on the morning of May 3d, 1863.

CHARGE 2d.—Neglect of duty, to the prejudice of good order and military discipline.

Specification.—In this, that Brigadier-General J. W. REVERE, U. S. Volunteers, commanding Excelsior (Second) Brigade, Second Division, Third Corps, did allow public property to the amount of 189 muskets, 178 sets of accoutrements, 259 bayonets, 28,440 rounds of small-arm ammunition, 1,779 knapsacks, 836 haversacks, 494 canteens, 2,000 shelter-tents, and fifty-five pioneer tools, in the service of his command, to be abandoned, and to fall into the hands of the enemy.

All this without orders from his superior officers at Chancellorsville, Virginia, on or about May 3d, 1863.

(Signed)　　　　H. EDWARD TREMAIN, *Major and A. D. C.*

Before pleading to the charges, the accused asked permission to introduce Brigadier-General BIRNEY, U. S. Volunteers, as his counsel, which was acceded to by the Court.

The accused then asked permission to introduce Captain CHESTER, Fifth Excelsior Regiment, to assist in recording testimony. This was also acceded to by the Court.

General Birney and Captain Chester then took their seats in the court-room. The accused then pleaded as follows :

To the Specification of 1st Charge. Not Guilty.

To 1st Charge. Not Guilty.

To the Specification of 2d Charge. Not Guilty.

To 2d Charge. Not Guilty.

Major-General DANIEL E. SICKLES, commanding Third Corps, a witness for the prosecution, duly sworn in the presence of the accused, testified as follows :

I commanded the Third Army Corps on May 3d; General Revere commanded the Second Brigade, Second Division of that corps. The orders that the Second Division had, which were communicated in person to General Berry, were to occupy the rifle-pits and intrenchments to the right and left of the plank-road between Chancellorsville and General Slocum's head-quarters on Friday. General Birney's division was to the left of General Berry, and in front of the house which I mentioned as General Slocum's head-quarters. When we retired from that position, I took a second position in rear of Chancellorsville, where I established my head-quarters, formed on the road leading to United States Ford, and where, through staff officers, I directed commanding officers of brigades and divisions to report to me with their commands. General Berry was killed before this last movement. The command of the Second Division devolved upon Brigadier-General Carr, to whom I communicated my orders. General Carr informed me, through a staff officer, that General Revere claimed the command of the division as senior; I did not recognize the claim of General Revere. Observing that the Second Brigade of that division (Revere's), and a portion of the Third Brigade (Mott's), did not report, I sent to General Carr for an explanation, and he reported that General Revere had taken his brigade, and he supposed a portion of the Third Brigade, to the rear. I directed him to investigate the matter at once, and direct General Revere to report with his command at the front. I sent some of my staff officers to find General Revere, with the same instructions. In the mean time, I supplied my troops with ammunition, and remained in that position an hour, or an hour and a half, until we moved to the third position, where we intrenched. General Revere not yet reporting, I sent staff officers to find him, and conduct his column to the position I was occupying. It was reported to me that they found him in the vicinity of United States Ford. One of my staff officers conducted him, and he got up with his column in the afternoon. I directed him to report to me in person for explanation, and he stated that he went down for ammunition. I told him his explanation was not satisfactory, and relieved him from command.

Ques. by Judge Advocate.—Did you give the accused any orders to march his brigade from the field?

Ans.—None.

Ques. by J. A.—Should orders to that or any other effect to him have come from you?

Ans.—Yes; and certainly with General Revere's views of his rank and command.

Accused wished to ask no questions of this witness.

Ques. by Court.—Was the division in question under fire, or engaged with the enemy, during the time the command of General Revere was leaving the field, as laid in the Specification?

Objected to by a member, and the Court was closed for deliberation. After discussion, it was decided to allow the question to be put. The Court was opened, and the decision announced, when the question was withdrawn by the Court.

Ques. by the Court.—Who is the senior, General Carr or General Revere?

Ans.—General Carr. In justice to General Revere I ought to state: I think that he might have been under the impression that he was senior, because, although General Carr was originally his senior, General Revere's appointment was confirmed by the Senate, and General Carr's appointment was not acted on. General Carr was subsequently reappointed, and the letter of reappointment bore date in March, '63. It was afterwards cancelled, and he was appointed from his original date, which re-established the relative rank, making Carr the senior. It was perhaps known to General Revere that General Carr's reappointment bore date in March, and not perhaps known to him that General Carr's original date had been given to him.

Colonel I. E. FARNUM, First Excelsior Regiment, a witness for the prosecution, duly sworn, testified as follows:

On the 3d of May I belonged to the Second Brigade, Second Division, Third Corps. I was commanding the First Excelsior Regiment,— General Joseph Revere commanding the brigade. On Sunday we were in line of battle to the right of the plank-road,—at an early hour in the morning we were attacked on our whole line. After firing for some considerable time, the enemy turned our left, and came upon the regiment that I commanded in such force that we were obliged to give way in common with the rest of the brigade. My regiment gave way with as much regularity as the dense wood would permit, and came into the open field near the White House. I there reformed what was left of my regiment. I then received an order, from an aide-de-camp on General Revere's staff, to move my regiment and form it on the right of the Fourth Excelsior, which was close by;—pending the execution of the order, I received another order to march with the balance of the brigade. We marched to the left of the United States Ford road, over to the breastworks that had been thrown up opposite there, facing Fredericksburg. The breastworks were filled with troops. There General Revere assumed command of the division, or of the regimental fragments of the division that were there. And marching by his orders, we struck a bee-line through the woods, striking the United States Ford road at a distance of about a mile and a quarter, I should suppose, from the White House. We were there ordered to form column of division at half distance at the side of the road, and were halted. In a very short time after we were in column of division, we were marched by a flank down the United States Ford road, to within a mile and a quarter from the brick house near the ford. We marched about two miles and a half from the White House. We were then halted, and the men were allowed to rest. Ammunition was sent for to supply the deficiencies of the troops, and distributed. The movements took place by order of General Revere. At the time I got the first order, I had just formed on the road and was collecting my regiment together. The enemy followed us up to the skirt of the woods, which left us a considerable piece of ground for us to pass over before I had reformed my regiment.

Ques. by J. A.—How far to the rear was the position where General Revere first reformed his brigade?

Ans.—About six or eight hundred yards.

Ques. by J. A.—When your regiment was marched away as you have described, by General Revere's orders, did you leave any public property behind?

Ans.—We did not leave property there,—the property had been left the day previous, and we had not recovered it—it was left within five hundred yards of the brick house at Chancellorsville.

Ques. by J. A.—How far to the rear did you proceed when you were finally halted?

Ans.—About two and a half miles from the scene of action. I am a bad judge of distance. I base my calculation upon my idea that Chancellorsville was three and a half to four miles by the road from the ford.

Ques. by J. A.—Can you specify what amount of property was left behind by your regiment?

Ans.—The knapsacks of all the men, and the principal part of the arms and accoutrements of the pioneer corps.

Ques. by J. A.—Could the brigade have been reformed sooner, or nearer to the scene of action than it was?

Ans.—There was room enough to have formed it almost anywhere. The brigade, according to my judgment, could not have been formed sooner than it was.

Ques. by accused.—State the hour, accurately as possible, on May 3d, that the Second Division ceased to engage the enemy and retired from the front line or position held by it in the morning?

Ans.—About half-past 8 A. M., as near as I can judge.

Ques. by accused.—Was or was not the distance marched by your brigade to the rear to reform, rendered necessary on account of the front being filled with troops waiting to go into action?

Ans.—It could not have been formed sooner, or in a more advantageous ground.

Ques. by accused.—State the number of troops, with as much accuracy as possible, that were under General Revere's command when he commenced the march to the rear, and were they in fit condition to engage the enemy?

Ans.—About 1,200 men; I should say they were not in a fit condition to engage the enemy, having expended their ammunition to a considerable extent.

Ques. by accused.—Were the knapsacks, shelter-tents, haversacks and pioneer tools of the entire division thrown off and abandoned on Saturday evening when the division went to the front under Major-General Berry, and has the loss of those articles been general throughout the division?

Ans.—I can only speak as to our own brigade. The whole brigade deposited their knapsacks on the afternoon of Saturday the 2d, General Berry was then in command of the division, and they were never resumed.

General Joseph B. Carr, a witness for the prosecution, duly sworn in the presence of the accused, testified as follows:

I belonged to the First Brigade, Second Division, Third Corps, on the 3d of May, 1863. The division was under command of General Berry, who was wounded and died about 7.26 A. M. of that day. I was then notified by the chief of staff that I was in command of the division. I took command of that portion of the division that was in my front, comprising the First and Third Brigades and part of the Second. After I took command of the division I saw nothing of the Second Brigade until they reported to me that afternoon about 4 o'clock in the rear of the White House. Colonel Farnum reported to me in command of the brigade. General Revere sent an aide or an orderly to me about 11 A. M., and ordered me to report to him near the United States Ford, so the aide said; I do not remember the name of the aide. I told my assistant adjutant-general to inform the aide that I was in command of the division, and sent word by the aide to General Revere to report to me with his command at the front at about 2 P. M. I sent a written order to General Revere to report with his command.

Ques. by accused.—At what hour on Sunday, May 3d, did the Second Division cease to engage the enemy, and retire from the front?

Ans.—About 8.50 A. M., I think, near 9 o'clock.

At 12.40 Court took a recess for half an hour; at 1.30 P. M. Court reassembled; members all present; Judge Advocate and accused also present.

Lieutenant-Colonel C. D. WESTBROOK, 120th New York Volunteers, a witness for the prosecution, duly sworn in the presence of the accused, testified as follows:

I was in command of my regiment on the 3d of May; it belongs to the Second Brigade, Second Division, Third Corps. The brigade fell back from the front, about, I should judge, 6.30 or 7 A. M. of that day; it fell back about half a mile, then the regiments formed near a battery. While our regiment was forming in a line with the battery, I received an order to fall back and join the brigade. I do not know by whom the order was given to me, but I think it was one of the staff officers of General Revere. We moved about a hundred yards to the rear of our then position and joined the other regiments of the brigade. I then received an order from General Revere to take the lead with my regiment and move in the direction of the ford; we crossed the United States Ford road or a road leading to the ford. We struck through the woods about a mile and a half, I should judge, and struck the road leading to the ford. We moved a little way down the road about a quarter of a mile; we halted and were supplied with ammunition there. I do not know where the ammunition came from. We remained there more than an hour, and then marched back again.

Ques. by J. A.—How far from the scene of action was the point to which you finally marched?

Ans.—About two miles and a half.

Ques. by J. A.—How far was the point you reached from the United States Ford?

Ans.—I can't say exactly; I should judge it was about a mile. I judge so because I saw a house which seemed to me to be a house we had passed on our march from the ford.

Ques. by J. A.—Did your regiment leave any public property behind it?

Ans.—We left our knapsacks; they were taken off on Friday, I think. There was a house to our right, and a little to our front at the time we took them off. We did not return to the point where we took off our knapsacks.

Ques. by J. A.—How far did the brigade retire from action before it was reformed?

Ans.—About half a mile, I should judge.

Ques. by J. A.—Was the Second Division engaged with the enemy at the time the brigade was retired and reformed?

Ans.—My regiment was engaged with the enemy and so were the regiments on my right and left. I thought so from their firing. We were in a thick wood.

Ques. by J. A.—Were there any other troops than the Second Brigade of your division with you when you were marched towards the ford as you have described?

Ans.—I think the 26th Pennsylvania was with us. That regiment belongs to the division but not to the brigade.

Ques. by accused.—Was or was not your regiment in fit condition to engage the enemy when marched to the rear under General Revere? How many men had you at the first roll-call during the halt?

Ans.—At the first roll-call we had 220 men, about two-thirds of the regiment, when first ordered to fall back from the position, where the regiment was reforming, we had about thirty or forty men. At the time we were ordered to move toward the ford I judge we had from a hundred to a hundred and fifty. The men had some ammunition, but they needed rest and food, and the companies were much disorganized; with these qualifications the men were fit to engage the enemy.

Ques. by accused.—At the halt made by your regiment did you or did you not receive orders from General Revere to collect your stragglers, obtain ammunition, and get your command in readiness for action?

Ans.—I did receive such orders.

Major M. W. Burns, 4th Regiment Excelsior Brigade (Second Brigade, Second Division, Third Corps), witness for the prosecution, duly sworn in the presence of the accused, testified as follows:

I was serving with my regiment on Sunday, the 3d of May. General Revere was in command of the brigade. On Sunday morning I received orders, I think, by an aide of General Berry to move my regiment to the extreme right, on the right of the 26th Pennsylvania. I moved my regiment and formed in line of battle. I was in line, I judge, three-quarters of an hour before the fighting commenced on my left, and did not fall back until the regiment on my left had fallen back. I fell back outside the woods at the White House. I then rallied my regiment and received orders, I think, from General Revere, to form by division in close column. I did so. We marched back through the woods and came out on the same road I had advanced on in coming from the United States Ford. On striking the road I took my adjutant's horse and rode back to the front; I there met an aide of General Sickles' staff, who said he had been sent with an order to the brigade to deploy and drive all the stragglers to the front. I went back and rejoined my regiment, and supplied them with all the ammunition they required. I understood the ammunition was ordered by General Revere, but do not know where it was brought from. From the point where we halted I could see the brick house near the ford. I know that portions of the division were engaged with the enemy at the time the regiment fell back. I received no orders to fall back. I do not know that the division was engaged when I fell back; it had been engaged and was driven back.

Ques. by J. A.—Did your regiment leave any public property behind it on leaving the field, and if so, where?

Ans.—Before going into the field I left the knapsacks, the arms, tools and slings of the pioneers, and a majority of the haversacks, near the Chancellor House. I left nothing on the field except what was left by wounded men.

At 2.45 P. M. the Court adjourned, to meet to-morrow at 10 A. M.

SECOND DAY.—May 14th.

Court met at 10.15. A. M.

Present.

1. Major-General W. S. HANCOCK, Volunteer Service.
2.   "   "   JOHN NEWTON,   "   "
3.   "   "   JAS. S. WADSWORTH, "   "
4.   "   "   W. T. H. BROOKS,   "   "
5.   "   "   A. A. HUMPHREYS,   "   "
6.   "   "   JOHN GIBBON,   "   "
7.   "   "   FRAS. C. BARLOW,   "   "
8.   "   "   R. B. AYRES,   "   "
9.   "   "   S. K. ZOOK,   "   "

Lieutenant-Colonel E. R. PLATT, *Judge Advocate*, also present. Accused and counsel also present. Proceedings of yesterday read over and approved. Major ROBERT L. BODINE, 26th Pennsylvania Volunteers, a witness for the prosecution, duly sworn in the presence of the accused, testified as follows:

My regiment belonged to the First Brigade, Second Division, Third Corps on the 3d of May. In the morning of that day my regiment was engaged in the fight in the front line, on the right of the Excelsior Brigade (Second Brigade), except one regiment, Major Burns, which was on my right. After the line became broken on our left, about 6 or 7 o'clock in the morning, we retired to the open ground in rear of the batteries, by order of Colonel Tilghman, who was then wounded. He then ordered me to take charge of the regiment, which I did, and reformed it. I marched it a short distance to where I saw parts of two regiments of our brigade. About five minutes had elapsed, when I was looking for General Carr, a gentleman rode up to me, I understood him to be General Revere's A. A. G., and told me I was under the command of General Revere. He had scarcely left when General Revere himself rode up, asked me what regiment it was, told me that General Berry had been killed and General Mott wounded, and that he was the senior officer and had command of the division; I signified my willingness to obey his orders. He told me to follow him; that he was going to move the division. We marched through the woods almost on a line with the road running to the ferry, and struck that road about a mile and a half, I think, from the breastworks, where we halted. After a short rest, we proceeded on down that road to within sight of the river—about a mile or a mile and a half, I do not think it was over a mile much from the river. We did not get out to the open ground, and could not see the river, but could see the banks of the river. We were not there long, and returned to the front that same afternoon.

Ques. by J. A.—Did you, before returning to the front, see General Revere, after his interview with you which you have described, and if so, where?

Ans.—I saw him at both halts; I saw him where we halted on the road, and saw him where we halted and turned back.

Ques. by J. A.—How far to the rear was the extreme point you reached in that direction?

Ans.—I do not know the exact distance. I suppose it was good four miles. I was told it was five miles to the river, and we were within a mile or mile and a half of the river.

Ques. by J. A.—Did your regiment leave any public property behind it on leaving the field?

Ans.—Yes, sir; all their knapsacks, all their haversacks, and all their overcoats.

Ques. by J. A.—Was the division in action when your regiment fell to the rear, and when General Revere told you he was in command of the division?

Ans.—It had just been in action. As far as I could ascertain, it had been forced to retire from the woods. When my regiment fell to the rear, the division was in action. I think the division was not in action when General Revere told me he was in command of the division.

Ques. by Accused.—When you marched to the rear under General Revere's order, how many men were in the ranks of your regiment, and were they in fit condition to engage the enemy?

Ans.—I had 310 men; the day previous I had 520 men; about twenty were detailed on other duty, which left me about 500 men. I think I could have given them a pretty good fight. The only thing that was the matter with them was that they were very hungry. They had eaten nothing since noon the day before (Saturday).

Ques. by Accused.—State from whom you received orders to leave the knapsacks, haversacks, and other property of your command on the field.

3

Ans.—General Carr first issued an order to leave every thing. General Berry repeated the order. That was Saturday afternoon.

Colonel N. B. McLaughlin, 1st Massachusetts Volunteers, a witness for the prosecution, duly sworn in the presence of the accused, testified as follows :

My regiment belonged to the First Brigade, Second Division, Third Corps, on the 3d of May.

Ques. by J. A.—On the morning of that day, did your regiment have its knapsacks and shelter-tents with it ?

Ans.—No.

Ques. by J. A.—Where was that property ? had it been left by order, and whose order ?

Ans.—It was left the night before. I received the order from General Carr. It was left in the woods, perhaps five or six hundred yards from where General Hooker had his head-quarters.

Ques. by J. A.—Were the knapsacks of the whole division left at the same place ?

Ans.—I can only speak for the regiment in front of me. Theirs were left.

Ques. by J. A.—Did your regiment recover its knapsacks, &c., which had been so left ?

Ans.—Part of them did. A part that stayed with me and the colors got their knapsacks. There was another part, that went with my major, that lost theirs.

Ques. by J. A.—Do you know where that part that was with the major went, and why they failed to recover their property ?

Ans.—I only know what the major told me himself when I took him to account. He reported to me officially.

Ques. by J. A.—What was his official report ?

Ans.—That he had attempted to reform a part of the regiment that followed him, and that, having done so, General Revere had ordered him to follow him ; that he was in command of the division, and that he had done so supposing it was correct.

Ques. by J. A.—Could that portion of the regiment which went off with the major have reformed where the colors were ?

Ans.—In explanation of the separation I will have to state that I was detached from the brigade, and placed in the front line with my regiment—my left resting on the plank-road, my right connecting with one of General Revere's regiments. The regiment on the left of me, a Maryland regiment, broke, and let them outflank me. My major then ran to me, telling me they were outflanking me. I directed him to remain in the rifle-pits we had made, as he was safer there than if he tried to leave, if they had outflanked him ; but the left wing followed him, when he ran over to me. I remained with the right wing a little longer. I do not know how he got out of the woods, or if he could have formed with the rest of the regiment. I know nothing to have prevented his forming with the rest. I think, however, if he had remained as I told him, he would have been captured, as they had already captured a section of guns, which was all that prevented their turning my left.

Ques. by J. A.—If the left wing under command of the major had reformed with the rest of the regiment, would that portion of the regiment have recovered its property?

Ans.—Yes, sir. .

Ques. by Accused.—State at what hour, as accurately as possible, Berry's division withdrew from the front and ceased to engage the enemy, on May 3d, 1863.

Ans.—I should say that the time we came out of the woods, whether they were withdrawn or not I cannot tell, was about half-past seven in the morning—from that to eight o'clock. I at least ceased to engage the enemy at that time. I saw portions of the division coming out of the woods at the same time I did. I attempted to rally, and General Carr moved us off the field.

At this point a member moved to have the Court cleared, which was accordingly done. After some discussion, the Court was reopened—the accused, his counsel, and the witness returned to the court-room.

Testimony of Colonel McLaughlin continued:

Ques. by Court.—Did you recover your knapsacks, and immediately upon your retiring from the first line; and did you find any difficulty in obtaining them at the place where you left them?

Ans.—We did recover them immediately upon retiring from the first line, and we had no difficulty whatever in obtaining them. When General Carr marched us off we marched immediately to our old camp.

Ques. by Court.—Did the portion of your command which recovered its knapsacks, retire by the White House, known as the Chancellor House on the map, or did it return by way of Chancellorsville?

Ans.—We retired direct to the White House, without passing by Chancellor House.

Ques. by Court.—How far was it from the White House to the point where the knapsacks of the division were left?

Ans.—I should say that it was perhaps 500 or 600 yards. It was about half-way between the two houses; it was on the left of the road in the woods.

Ques. by Court.—How far from the point where General Revere's command was first re-formed was it to the point where you formed that part of your regiment referred to, which obtained their knapsacks?

Ans.—I know nothing about that. I did not see General Revere's command.

Ques. by Court.—Do you know where the knapsacks of General Revere's command had been put the evening before?

Ans.—I do not. His command lay in front of me; but I don't know where his knapsacks were.

Ques. by Court.—What kind of fire were your men subjected to when they recovered their knapsacks?

Ans.—They were shelling the plain in front of the woods where the knapsacks were; that was the only fire.

Ques. by Court.—Did you recover your knapsacks in retiring from your position in line of battle on your way to the White House, or did you return from the White House to get them, and about what time did you recover them?

Ans.—We recovered them on our way to the White House, about eight o'clock, or shortly after eight.

Ques. by Accused.—How many knapsacks did you recover?

Ans.—About half my command—probably about 160, or 175 perhaps; all the men with me got their knapsacks.

Captain GEORGE LE FORT, Fourth Excelsior Regiment, Acting Assistant Inspector-General, Second Brigade, Second Division, Third Corps, a witness for the prosecution, duly sworn in the presence of the accused, testified as follows:

I made an inspection of the brigade, I think on the 9th of May, at the present camp of the brigade, near Falmouth, Va. I found a certain amount of property missing. (Witness refers to memorandum to refresh his memory.) The following articles were missing:

> 189 muskets,
> 259 bayonets,
> 178 sets of equipments,
> 1,779 knapsacks,
> 836 haversacks,
> 494 canteens,
> 2,002 pieces of shelter-tent,
>   41 axes and slings,
>   10 spades and slings.

Ques. by J. A.—Do you know how this property was lost?
Ans.—No, sir.

Ques. by Accused.—How do you know that the described property was missing? Had you inspected the brigade previous to the time mentioned, or have you personal knowledge that the described property ever had been issued to the command?

Ans.—I ascertained from the commandants of companies and from personal inspection ; I had not inspected the brigade previously to the time mentioned. I had no personal knowledge that the property had been issued to the command.

PROSECUTION CLOSED.

At 12.45 P. M., Court took a recess for half an hour.

At 1.15 P. M., Court reassembled. All present—accused and counsel also present.

Major JOHN P. VINKELMEIER, Assistant Adjutant-General Second Brigade, Second Division, Third Corps, witness for defence, duly sworn in the presence of the accused, testified as follows :

Ques. by Accused.—State your name, rank, and duties on the 3d of May, 1863.

Ans.—John P. Vinkelmeier, Major, and Assistant Adjutant-General Second Brigade, Second Division, Third Corps. I held that position on the 3d of May.

Ques. by Accused.—State, if you know, the movements of Revere's brigade, and other troops of which General Revere assumed command on the 3d of May, 1863.

Ans.—We stood under fire until seven A. M., and after the enemy ceased to fire we fell back, meeting on the way the troops ordered to the front ; we came down to what they call White House, near General French's head-quarters. General Revere ordered me and the other staff officers to collect the fragments of the scattered regiments. After a great deal of effort, I succeeded in collecting about 600 or 800 men. General Revere reported with these men to General French, on the ground. General French ordered him to occupy the rifle-pits south of the plank-road. When marching up to the rifle-pits we found them occupied by other troops already. General Revere ordered then the regimental commanders to him, and informed them that he intended to fall back in order to collect the stragglers, our men being very much' exhausted, and almost without ammunition. We marched back through the woods to the first open place we could reach, where General Revere directed me to order details to pick up stragglers, and ordered the ammunition train up,—in the mean time affording our men a little rest, and preparing them for marching to the front again. The detail was made by me, and the train ordered. We succeeded in collecting stragglers, and the train arrived about an hour afterwards, or so. Ammunition was distributed, when General Revere, anxious to get our troops back again, ordered them to fall in, and marched to the front. Our men had scarcely time to prepare what little provisions they had for eating.

We came near the head-quarters of General Sickles some time between two and three. When about half or three-quarters of a mile distant from those head-quarters, we met Captain Chester, bringing an order from General Sickles for General Revere to return.

Ques. by Accused.—Under whose order, and when, were the troops of Revere's brigade stripped of knapsacks, haversacks, &c., for the fight, and was it or was it not possible afterwards to recover them?

Ans.—The order was given by a staff officer of General Berry, with the intention of preparing our troops for light marching order, Saturday evening, before we marched up the plank-road. They were to be left in charge of the pioneers and the musicians. In my opinion it was impossible afterwards to recover them, the brigade being on the right, and the ground being too much occupied and intersected by other troops as well as the advancing enemy, as well as on account of the heavy cannon firing on the part of the enemy.

Ques. by J. A.—Was the order you say you met Captain Chester taking to you, the first one received to return to the front?

Ans.—It was the first I was aware of. I was with General Revere all the time, and would have known if any had been brought. Subsequently an order to the same effect was brought by Lieutenant Banks, of General Sickles' staff.

Ques. by Court.—How near to the United States Ford did General Revere take his command?

Ans.—About a mile and a half or two miles from the ford, in my opinion.

Ques. by Court.—Where was the ammunition train that you speak of ordered from?

Ans.—I suppose it was from the front. I don't know the location of the train; to judge from the direction the train arrived, I believe it came from the front.

Lieutenant CHARLES R. PAUL, 15th New Jersey Volunteers, and aide-de-camp to General Revere, witness for the defence, duly sworn in the presence of the accused, testified as follows:

Ques.—State your name, rank, and your duties on the 3d of May, 1863.

Ans.—Charles R. Paul, Second Lieutenant 15th New Jersey, and aide-de-camp to General Revere.

Ques. by Accused.—Give as fully as possible the movements of Revere's brigade, and of the troops over which General Revere assumed command on the 3d of May, 1863.

Ans.—The brigade formed line of battle on the right of the first brigade of the division on the afternoon of the 2d of May. On the morning of the 3d of May, at daylight, the enemy advanced on our front; after some time they turned our left flank. The brigade then fell back in the rear of General French's command, where the regiments were gathered together and formed in line. We then retired through the woods, and struck the road leading to White House at an old deserted rebel camp. The command was halted; orders sent to the different regiments to send out details and gather together their stragglers. Ammunition was sent for and furnished to the troops. The general also sent to the river for provisions for the men. There being some delay in obtaining them, he decided not to wait, and marched his command to the front. When we were about two-thirds between the rebel camp and the White House, we met an aide from General Sickles, with orders for General Revere to bring the command to the front.

Ques. by Accused.—When General Revere commenced to move his command to the rear, had or had not Berry's division ceased to engage the enemy?

Ans.—It had ceased to engage the enemy. When reformed in rear of French's division, we did not engage the enemy after we were repulsed from the woods.

Ques. by Accused.—State under whose orders the knapsacks, shelter-tents, and other property of Revere's brigade were stripped off, and whether the position of the enemy and condition of brigade admitted of their repossession.

Ans.—They were taken off by order of General Berry; they were on the left of our position, and from the direction we came out of the woods it was impossible, in my opinion, to regain possession of them.

Ques. by J. A.—You say ammunition was sent for. Where was it sent for?

Ans.—To the ford.

Ques. by Court.—Who was the aide from General Sickles that met you on the road returning? And do you know whether the order for the command to return, delivered by him, was the first orders received from General Sickles to that effect? From what point was the ammunition received that was issued to the troops?

Ans.—Lieutenant Banks was the aide. Captain Chester had a similar order. We were resting on the road when he brought it. The ammunition was received from the ford. I saw the train come in, and was present when it was issued; it came from the ford.

Ques. by Court.—Was any order received by General Revere from General Carr or any other superior officer, while you were in camp near the ford, to return to the front?

Ans.—Not to my knowledge.

Ques. by Court.—Was the ammunition distributed to the brigade that belonging to your division, or was it some other ammunition?

Ans.—I do not know.

The accused was asked if he had any more witnesses to call, or any other defence to offer, to which he replied in the negative.

The Court was then cleared, and, after mature deliberation on the evidence adduced, found the accused, Brigadier-General JOSEPH W. REVERE, as follows:

Of the Specification First Charge—Guilty, except the words, "while said division was engaged with the enemy at Chancellorsville, Virginia, did march his command an unnecessary distance to the rear to reform it, and" "then" and "to United States Ford, about five miles from the scene of action," substituting for the latter clause, "to about three miles from the scene of action, towards United States Ford."

Of the First Charge—*Not Guilty*, but *Guilty* of conduct to the prejudice of good order and military discipline.

Of the Specification to Second Charge—Not Guilty.

Of Second Charge—Not Guilty.

And the Court does therefore sentence him, Brigadier-General JOSEPH W. REVERE, United States Volunteers, to be dismissed from the military service of the United States.

W. S. HANCOCK,

Major-General United States Volunteers,

President of Court.

E. R. PLATT, *Lieutenant-Colonel and Judge Advocate.*

Approved:

JOSEPH HOOKER, *Major-General Commanding.*

At 3.30 P. M. the Court adjourned, to meet at 10 A. M. to-morrow.

THIRD DAY.—May 15th, 1863.

At 10 A. M. Court met.

Present.

1. Major-General W. S. HANCOCK, Volunteer Service.
2. "   "   JOHN NEWTON,   "   "
3. Brig.-General JAS. S. WADSWORTH, "   "
4. "   "   W. T. H. BROOKS,   "   "
5. "   "   A. A. HUMPHREYS,   "   "
6. "   "   JOHN GIBBONS,   "   "
7. "   "   R. B. AYRES,   "   "
8. "   "   S. K. ZOOK,   "   "

Lieutenant-Colonel E. R. PLATT, *Judge Advocate,* also present. General Barlow absent.

Proceedings of yesterday read over and approved.

There being no further business before the Court, it adjourned (*sine die*).

W. S. HANCOCK,
Major-General United States Volunteers,
President of Court.

E. R. PLATT, *Lieutenant-Colonel and Judge Advocate.*

HEAD-QUARTERS ARMY OF THE POTOMAC, }
May 15th, 1863. }

The proceedings in the case of General Revere are approved ; and under the Sixty-fifth Article of War, the record in the case is respectfully forwarded for the action of the President of the United States.

JOSEPH HOOKER,
Major-General Commanding.

APPENDIX No. II.

Copy of Brigadier-General Revere's Report of Operations.

SECOND DIVISION, THIRD CORPS. }
HEAD-QUARTERS EXCELSIOR SECOND BRIGADE, }
CAMP NEAR FALMOUTH, VA., *May 9th,* 1863. }

Lieutenant-Colonel O. H. HART,
Assistant Adjutant-General Third Army Corps:

COLONEL :—I have the honor respectfully to report the operations of the brigade during the last few days, as follows :

On the 28th of April, 1863, in pursuance of orders from Division Head-Quarters, at 3.30 P. M. we left our encampment and bivouacked for the night near the Rappahannock, below Fredericksburg, near Skinker's Bend. The next day we moved about one mile nearer the river, and again bivouacked for the night.

On the 30th April again followed the division column in company with the whole Third Corps, to the vicinity of the United States Ford of the Rappahannock, and bivouacked.

The next day, May 1st, 1863, we crossed the river on the pontoon bridge, and proceeded about one and a half miles from the ford, where we were placed in position to the right of the road, with a strong picket-guard of the brigade in our front facing westwardly, but before we had completed the disposition of the troops, were ordered to proceed immediately to the front at Chancellorsville, which we did, reaching that place about 5 p. m., and finding our forces hotly engaged with the enemy in the advance. We were posted in mass as a reserve on the left of the road, near the brick hotel, and again bivouacked under arms.

Here we remained until about 5 p. m. Saturday, May 2d, although under arms from several alerts which occurred in the course of the day, the enemy passing meanwhile in great force from the left to the right of our position. At that hour the enemy attacked our right with a tremendous assault, and the whole Eleventh Corps, upon which it was made, gave way, and we were hurried up to intercept their fugitives and repel the enemy.

We moved forward on the road, this brigade leading, and the major-general commanding the division at our head, first brigade in our rear, meeting fugitives, ambulances, batteries, caissons, limbers, &c., hurrying to the rear, of the troops which had broken.

I received orders to cover the road on each side, and had already deployed the 3d Excelsior to the right, and the 4th Excelsior to the left of the road, when other orders were given to the rear regiments, and the whole brigade was dispersed in the thick woods and undergrowth on the right of the plank-road, in a short time, no two regiments joining together.

After considerable efforts on the part of myself and my staff, we succeeded in joining the regiments again, and forming a line of battle in the dense woods, which extended in a semicircular form from the plank-road to a woods road on the right, in the following order, commencing on the right: 26th Pennsylvania, 3d Excelsior, 1st Excelsior, 2d Excelsior, 120th New York, 5th Excelsior, 1st Massachussetts (I believe), and a Maryland regiment resting on the plank-road to Orange Court House. The 4th Excelsior did not join the brigade until the next morning, having been placed on the left of the plank-road by order of General Berry.

Before being entirely formed we received orders to charge the enemy with the bayonet, but no enemy appeared just then in our front.

Immediately I had formed my line I sent out scouts and deployed skirmishers in advance, who reported the enemy's pickets in front, and heavy masses of infantry in their rear.

During the night we succeeded in forming a line of long breastworks with abatis in front, and had frequent alarms, our pickets being several times driven in.

We also captured a captain and some twenty privates of the enemy, all of whom agreed in reporting that General A. P. Hill was in our front with a large force, and that the enemy's forces were being massed both on our left and to the right, with a view of gaining possession of the cross-roads, and of getting between us and our communications with the river at the same time.

I went to the rear during the night, but found no second line there. I however discovered a break of half a mile from our right to the next force at White House (there being no troops between the two points).

At early daylight the enemy drove in our pickets, and commenced the battle with a terrific fire of artillery and musketry, while his sharpshooters were also actively engaged. Our gallant soldiers, however, undauntedly returned their fire from behind their low defences, and defiantly answered their savage yells by hearty cheering, and for several hours maintained their position, when the enemy having turned our left flank and enfiladed the breastwork, the brigade broke off gradually, regiment after regiment, from the left, and reluctantly yielded their ground to a vastly superior force, who however were well punished by our men.

Owing to the practice of the enemy firing so low, the breastwork was a great protection, which will account for the comparatively small number of casualties in the brigade. Our brigade, however, lost all their knapsacks, blankets, shelters, and rations which were left at the bivouac near the cross-roads, and which we were forced to abandon during the enemy's assault on our position.

I here found that I was the senior officer of the division present, General Berry having been killed, and General Mott wounded.

On reaching the main road near the White House, in the rear of the retiring troops, I was joined by the Fourth Excelsior, and succeeded in collecting together some five or six hundred men from almost every regiment of the division, and with them reported to Brigadier-General French, who commanded at that point with his division, and asked for instructions. He designated to me a line of abatis and breastworks facing to the left, as a suitable place to occupy, but on arriving at them I found them lined with troops, and to put more there would be superfluous.

In fact, the whole place was covered with troops; and as a constant stream of stragglers was going to the rear by the main road, I decided to intercept them, by striking a straight course by compass through the woods from that point towards the ford, where I knew I should strike the main road, nearly midway, and be in a position to catch those on each side of the road.

I should also be in a position to go to either flank, as I might be directed, where our services would be required the most, and besides, have the opportunity to renew our exhausted ammunition, rest the troops, and recruit our thinned out ranks. On arriving at the point aimed at, on the high road, I halted the column, and immediately sent out officers from all the regiments present to collect the stragglers from the vicinity, and ordered ammunition to be procured and served out to the men, which was done.

At noon I called for reports from the regiments, and found that there were present for duty as follows, viz :

1st Excelsior, 210.	120th New York, 224.
2d Excelsior, 150.	1st Massachusetts, 80.
3d Excelsior, 204.	15th Massachusetts, 74.
4th Excelsior, 282.	26th Pennsylvania, 354.
5th Excelsior, 137.	

Aggregate, 1,715 officers and men.

All having been supplied with ammunition, refreshed, rested, and fitted again to take the field, I led the division towards the front, increasing our force at every rod of the road. At this time, having heard that the Third Brigade was collected close by the ford, I sent back one of my aides, Lieutenant Belger, to bring them up to join that part of the division then with me. Lieutenant Belger succeeded in collecting upwards of three hundred men of the different divisions of the corps, having been directed to do so by Lieutenant Colonel Hart, at United States Ford.

Arrived at the front at the head of about 2,000 men of the division, at 2.30 P. M. I reported to Major-General Sickles, commanding Third Corps, who relieved me from the command, having previously turned over the command of this brigade to Colonel J. Egbert Farnum, 1st Excelsior regiment.

Where all performed their duty nobly and gallantly, both officers and soldiers, it would be invidious to particularize ; but I would respectfully beg leave to mention the officers of my staff, Major John P. Vinkelmeier especially, for his valuable services in holding the command in hand, and carrying out my orders ; also Captain Young, who was wounded, and my aides-de-camp, Lieutenants Crofts, Paul, and Belger.

I regret deeply to say, that the brave Colonel William O. Stevens, of the 3d Excelsior, is either killed, or wounded and a prisoner ; and Lieutenant-Colonel Lounsbury and Major Alles, 5th Excelsior, are grievously wounded.

I would also respectfully call your attention to the regimental reports herewith enclosed, for particulars as to the meritorious conduct of the officers and men therein particularized, and who deserve promotion for their well-timed gallantry.

I subjoin a list of the casualties in the brigade, and remain, Colonel,

Very respectfully, your most obedient servant,

J. W. REVERE, *Brigadier-General.*

APPENDIX No. III.

The imminence of this danger from an attack upon our right at the river, and the confidence with which its result was anticipated by the rebel commanders, appear from the facts stated in the following extracts.

[Extract from the Detroit Free Press.]

"Captain William D. Wilkins, of the staff of General A. S. Williams, commanding a division of the Twelfth Corps, who was wounded and taken prisoner in the battle of Chancellorsville, communicates some interesting particulars of that battle.

"He was placed in charge of a guard, who took him a short distance to the rear, and to the plank-road, where he met General Jackson and his staff. Jackson had at this time formed a column of attack on the plank-road, with the design of flanking our army and obtaining possession of the United States Ford road, which would have undoubtedly resulted in the total annihilation of our army.

"The column consisted of upwards of 15,000 men, massed in columns of sections, having three batteries of artillery on the flank. •

    *   *   *   *   *   • *

"An officer of Jackson's staff subsequently stated that it was about fifteen minutes after this that General Jackson and staff advanced to the front to reconnoitre our position, having accomplished which he returned by a different path towards his own men, who, mistaking his approach for that of a party of our cavalry, fired upon him, killing and wounding four of his staff, and wounding Jackson."

[Extract from the New York Times.]

HEAD-QUARTERS ARMY OF THE POTOMAC,
May 23, 1863.

"Lieutenant Thomas J. Leigh, aide-de-camp to Brigadier-General Ward, commanding the Second Brigade of Birney's Division, Third

Corps, was taken prisoner by the enemy on the night of Saturday, the 2d instant.

"He had just returned from Richmond on parole, and gives some interesting statements of the rebel dispositions during the battle of Sunday, the 2d instant.

*   *   *   *   *   *   *

"As soon as taken, Lieutenant Leigh was sent to the rear, under the impression that he was a Union surgeon. This was between 12 and 1 o'clock Sunday morning. The enemy were then massed on the Orange County plank-road, about 30,000 strong, formed in five lines of battle, the right of the lines resting on the plank-road, their artillery in position on the north side of the road, where General Howard's head-quarters had been.

*   *   *   *   *   *   *

"During the whole of that night the rebel force was being strengthened by fresh arrivals of troops."

[*Extract from the Richmond Enquirer*—May 13th, 1863.]

"General Jackson, having gone some distance in front of the line of skirmishers on Saturday evening, was returning about 8 o'clock, attended by his staff and part of his couriers. The cavalcade was in the darkness of the night mistaken for a body of the enemy's cavalry, and fired upon by a regiment of his own corps.

*   *   *   *   .   *   *   *

"The operation (of amputation) was performed while he was under the influence of chloroform, and was borne well. * * * He sent for Mrs. Jackson, asked immediately about the battle, spoke cheerfully of the result, and said, 'If I had not been wounded, or had an hour more of daylight, I would have cut off the enemy from the road to the United States Ford, and we should have had them entirely surrounded, and they would have been obliged to surrender, or cut their way out. They had no other alternative.'"

APPENDIX No. IV.

HEAD-QUARTERS THIRD ARMY CORPS,
May 3d, 1863.

Brigadier-General REVERE,
    Commanding Excelsior Brigade, Second Division :

GENERAL :—General Sickles directs that you report immediately the authority under which you moved your brigade to the rear this morning.

I am, general, yours respectfully,

J. HAYDEN,
Lieutenant-Colonel and Assistant Adjutant-General.

ANSWER.

HEAD-QUARTERS EXCELSIOR BRIGADE, ⎰
IN THE FIELD, *May* 3d, 1863, 2.30 P. M. ⎱

Lieutenant-Colonel J. HAYDEN,
    Acting Assistant Adjutant-General, &c. :

COLONEL :—I have the honor to state that after my brigade had left the field this morning, I found myself the senior officer of the division present; and after rallying and forming the broken command, who were almost without ammunition and quite out of rations, I moved them down the road for the purpose of reorganizing and bringing them back to the field comparatively fresh, after consulting the commanding officers of the regiment present. I did not act under any orders, but did as seemed best to me under the circumstances.

This movement commenced about eight A. M., and I returned at two P. M., with parts of nearly every regiment in the division, having received numerous augmentations on the march, and with renewed ammunition.   I have the honor to be,

Very respectfully, your obedient serv't,

J. W. REVERE, *Brigadier-General.*

APPENDIX No. V.

HEAD-QUARTERS FIRST REGIMENT, EXCELSIOR BRIGADE,
CAMP NEAR FALMOUTH, VA., *May 20th*, 1863.

GENERAL :—My attention having been called to certain articles in the
New York City newspapers, which seem to reflect upon your courage,
and which distort your actions at a certain point of the brigade's his-
tory, I beg to respectfully state, that so far as your personal courage
and soldierly attributes are concerned, I have never heard officer or
man question them. Of a certainty I know, that when the fire was
warm, you were beside me calmly, and without any evidence of any
other sentiment than that which actuated the whole command, awaiting
some decisive movement. This much I know, as your next ranking
officer on the field. As to the movements that were subsequently
made, when the fighting was over, I do not feel called upon to express
an opinion, as it has been made the business of a General Court-Martial; but for the careless and inconsiderate slanders that have been
circulated, affecting you as a brave man, and an honorable soldier, I
am with you responsible.   Very respectfully,

Your obedient serv't,

J. EGBERT FARNUM.

The undersigned, field and staff officers of the regiments composing
the Excelsior Brigade, having been present at the battle of Chancellorsville, while the brigade was under the command of General Revere,
cordially indorse the above statement of Colonel J. Egbert Farnum.

> THOMAS RAFFERTY, *Major 2d Excelsior Regiment.*
> JOHN LEONARD, *Major 3d Excelsior Regiment.*
> N. WM. BURNS, *Major 4th Excelsior Regiment.*
> C. D. WESTBROOK, *Lieutenant-Colonel 120th New York Regiment.*
> T. EVELYN TYLER, *Captain Commanding 5th Excelsior Regiment.*
> J. P. VINKELMEIER, *Major, and Assistant Adjutant-General Excel-
> sior Brigade.*
> J. ELLIOTT CROFTS, *Lieutenant and A. D. C.*
> CHARLES R. PAUL, *Lieutenant and A. D. C.*

To Brigadier-General JOS. W. REVERE.

9 783337 733889